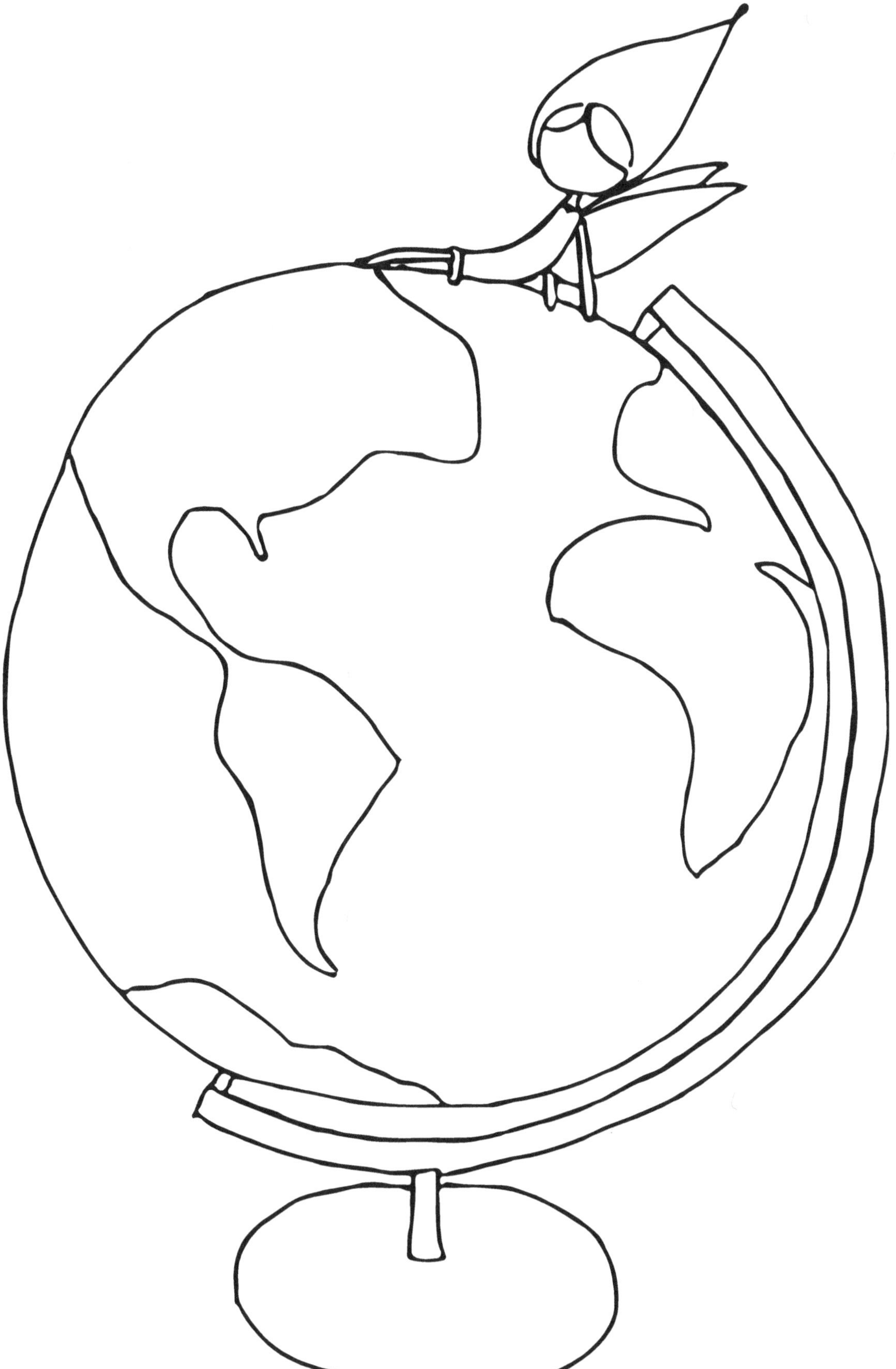

GOT MILK

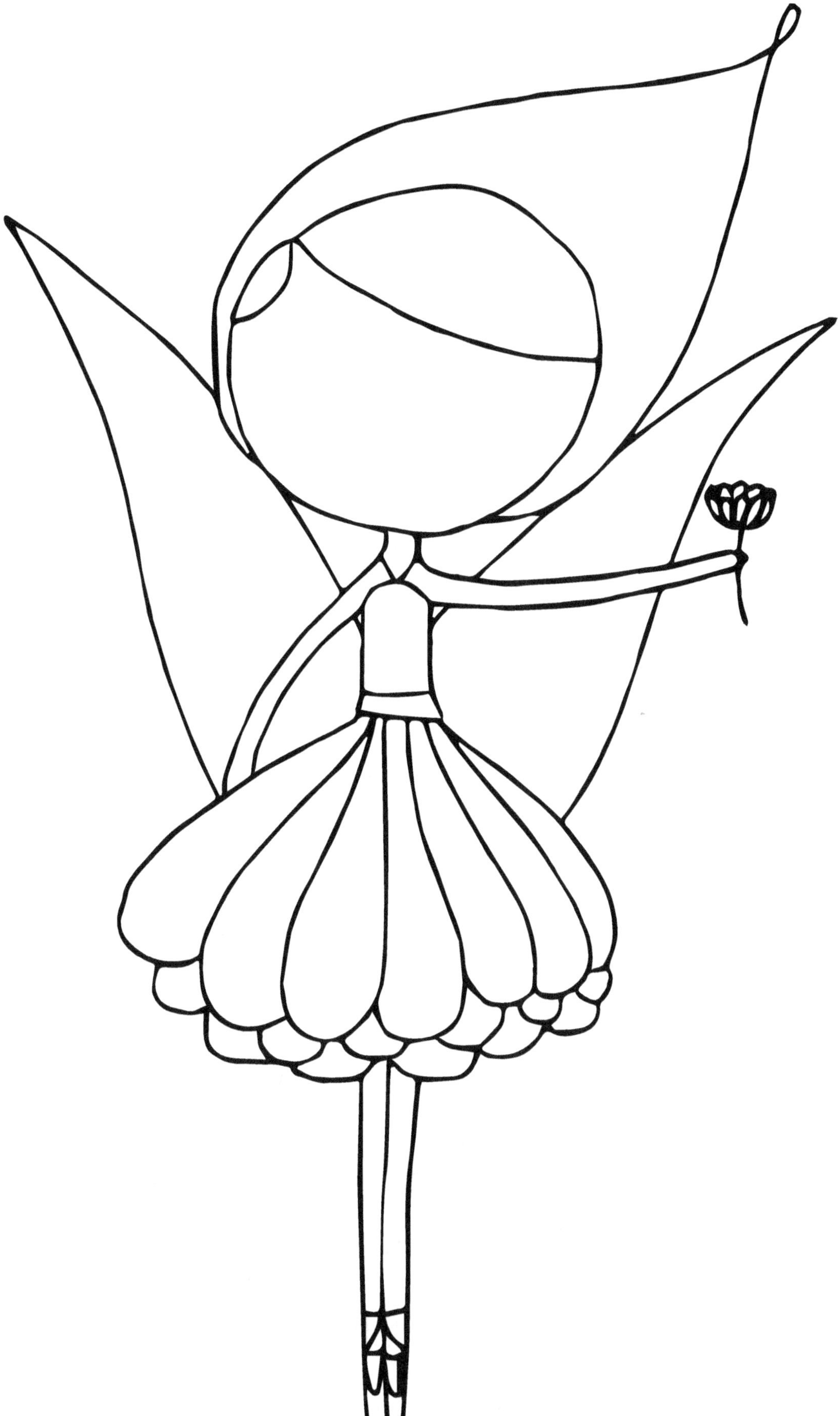

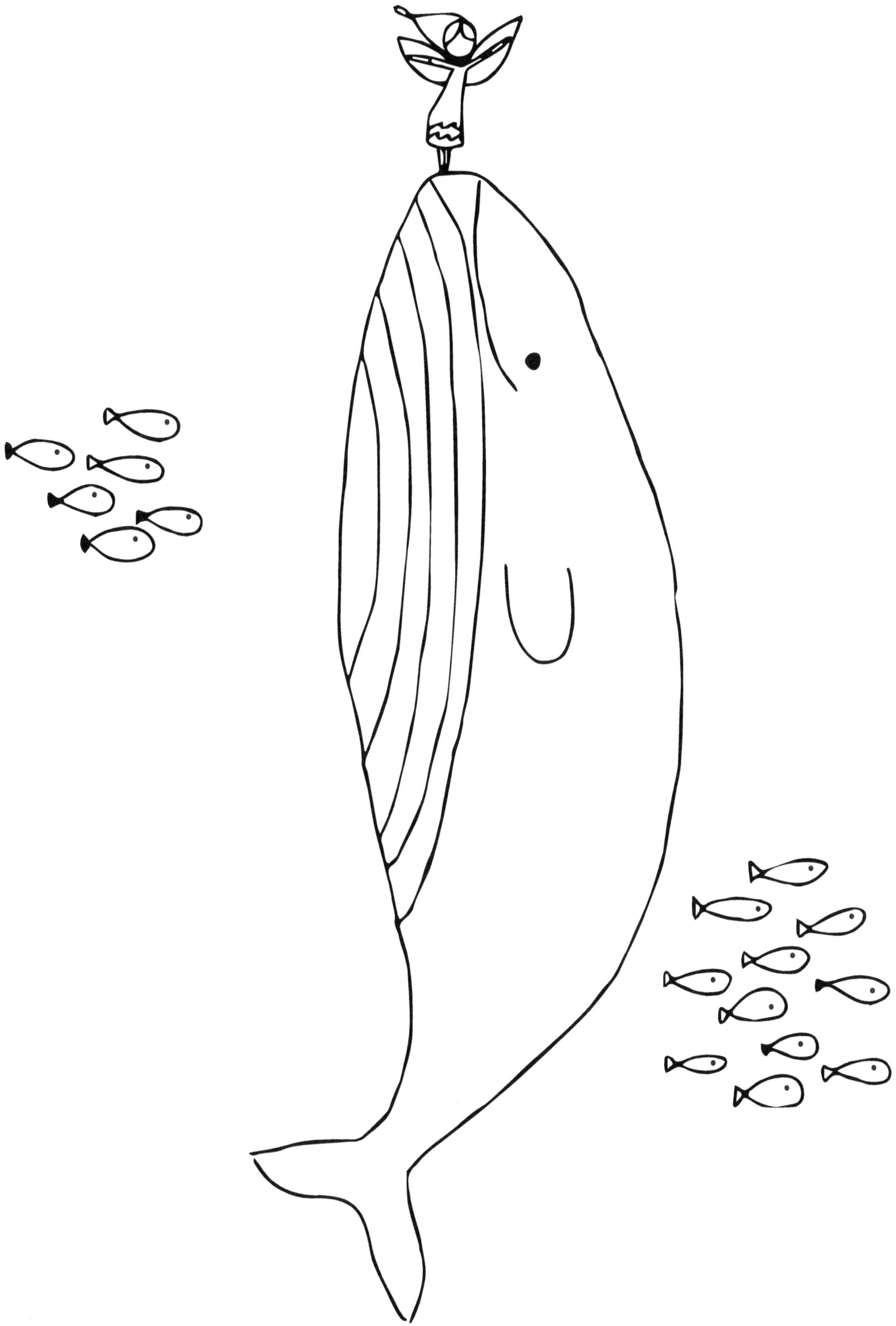

GOT MILK

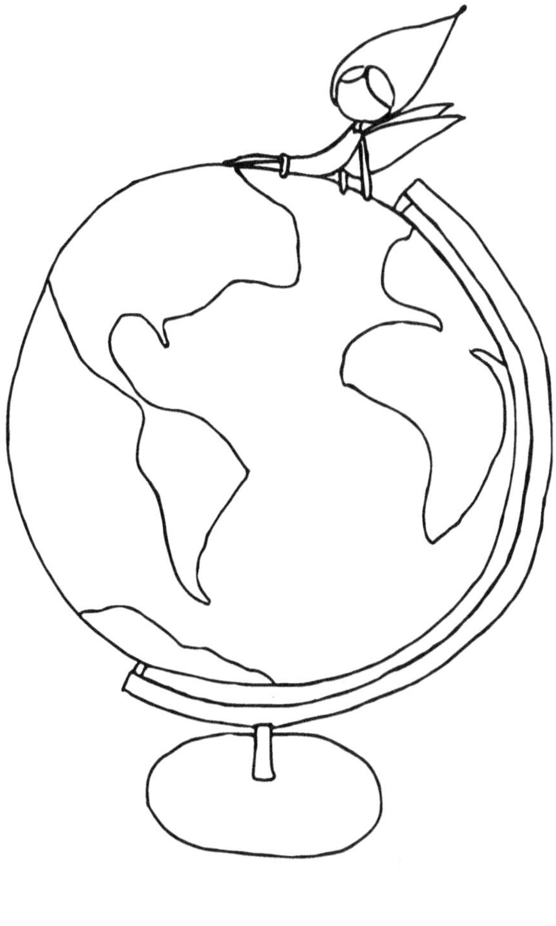

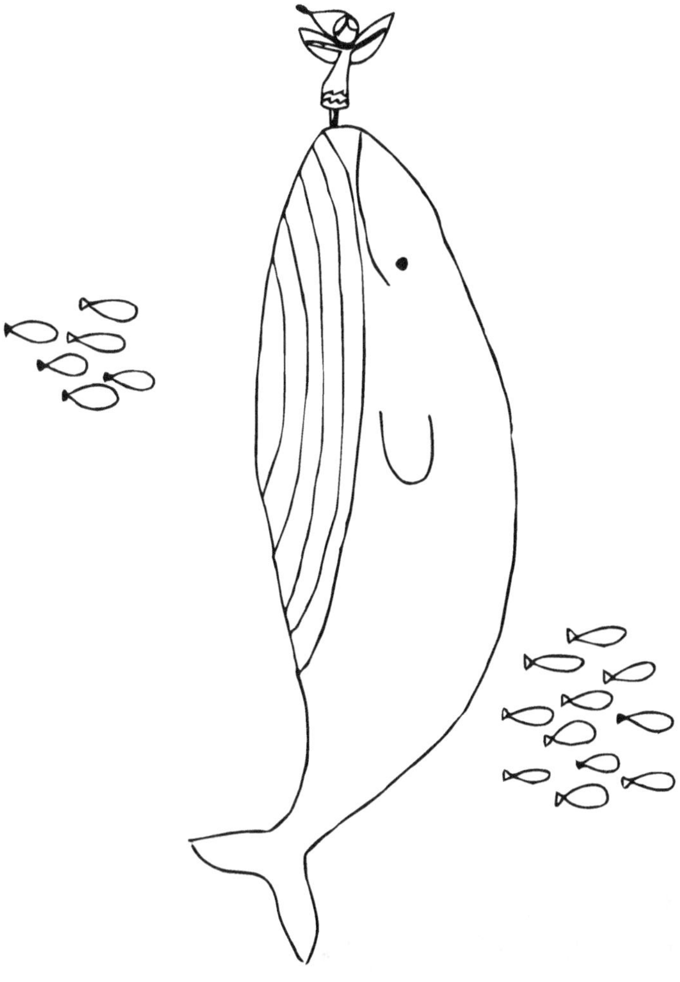

www.ingramcontent.com/pod-product-compliance
Lightning Source LLC
Chambersburg PA
CBHW051949280526
45789CB00009B/3225